Forgiveness

Living Out the High Calling of Our Faith

By Clay Gentry

© 2024 Spiritbuilding Publishers.
All rights reserved. No part of this book may be reproduced in any form without the written permission of the publisher.

Published by
Spiritbuilding Publishers
9700 Ferry Road, Waynesville, Ohio 45068

FORGIVENESS
Living Out the High Calling of Our Faith
By Clay Gentry

ISBN: 978-1-964805-03-0

Spiritbuilding
PUBLISHERS

spiritbuilding.com

Table of Contents

Introduction	Forgiveness	1
Lesson 1	Our Forgiving Father	4
Lesson 2	Our Need for Forgiveness	8
Lesson 3	Confessing Our Sins	12
Lesson 4	Accepting God's Forgiveness	16
Lesson 5	Saying I'm Sorry	21
Lesson 6	Saying You Hurt Me	25
Lesson 7	The Power of a Forgiving Spirit	29
Lesson 8	The Danger of an Unforgiving Spirit	33

Introduction

Forgiveness

Living Out the High Calling of Our Faith

Hurt. Anger. Pain. Grief. Agony. Disbelief. Sorrow. These and a hundred different other words describe the powerful feelings that naturally flood our hearts when someone has wronged us. As common as they may be, if left unchecked, these emotions can easily mutate into the gravely destructive disease of bitterness. The only antidote for such a spiritually fatal ailment is ... forgiveness.

The truth is we all need forgiveness. The apostle Paul declared, "All have sinned and fall short of the glory of God" (Romans 3:23). It then is painfully clear that we all have incurred an enormous debt of sin to God. However, the sum of that debt was graciously paid in full by God through the sacrifice of His own Son, Jesus. The penalty we deserve was paid by our Lord.

As Christians we celebrate the forgiveness we receive from our Father, but the rub comes from other people. It's the apostle Paul who charges us to, "Be kind to one another, tenderhearted, forgiving one another, as God in Christ forgave you" (Ephesians 4:32). Surely, those who have been forgiven so much by God should, of all people, forgive the offenses committed against them right? One would think, but even the saintliest of saints can struggle to forgive those who have wronged them. The fact of the matter is, how we deal with those who wrong us is a matter of spiritual life or death. The goal of this series is to empower us to live out the high calling of our faith; to forgive as we have been forgiven (cf. Matthew 6:12).

Throughout our lessons we'll explore the various facets of forgiveness in light of the scriptures. There won't be any magic words or secret formulas to learn. In fact, it's unlikely that we'll uncover many, if any, profound or new insights. Simply stated, forgiveness is not a method to be learned, but a truth to be lived. For most Christians, the problem isn't that we don't know the truth about forgiveness, it's that we don't practice it as we should. To encourage us to be more forgiving the course of our study will be two-fold:

God's Forgiveness of Us:
1. Our Forgiving Father (Luke 15:1–32)
2. Our Need for Forgiveness (Ephesians 2:1–10)
3. Confessing Our Sins (1 John 1:5–2:2)
4. Accepting Our Forgiveness (Psalms 32, 51)

Forgiving One Another:
5. Saying I'm Sorry (Matthew 5:21–26)
6. Saying You Hurt Me (Matthew 18:15–20)
7. The Power of a Forgiving Spirit (Romans 12:14, 17–21)
8. The Danger of an Unforgiving Spirit (Matthew 18:21–35)

It has been said that forgiveness is like a door leading to peace and joy. But it's a small door, and it can't be entered without stooping—or kneeling. Yet, if we're willing to humble ourselves and pass through that door, joy and peace awaits us on the other side. I'm truly convinced that when a person forgives another the transformation power of the gospel of grace is at work. Friends, this dark dying world needs more believers who will freely share God's grace and thereby bring more joy and peace into the lives of others.

It's my prayer, that as we search the scriptures together, our hearts will be open and receptive to God's word concerning the grace of forgiveness and that we will be divinely inspired to live out these truths in our lives.

—Clay Gentry

Lesson 1

Our Forgiving Father

Luke 15:1–32

Every morning the old man would rise, wondering if this day would be the day his broken-heart would heal. During the day, while working out in the fields, he would wishfully study any passerby looking for a certain face. Then in the cool of the evening, he would sit on his porch, longingly look out the gate and down the road, hoping to catch a glimpse of a figure headed home.

Then one day he saw him, a thin, ragged young man, with tattered clothes and the weary, disheveled look of a hard-worn traveler turning in from the road. Instantly the father knew it was the boy he had been waiting for all this time. With a sudden burst of excitement and desperate anticipation, the old man did something no one expected—he ran to lovingly embrace his son.

Jesus' story of the prodigal son never fails to move our hearts with amazement and wonder. Perhaps it's because we know this story all too well since it's about us. Even though we've squandered our Father's gifts and ignored His wishes, He runs to welcome us home and celebrate our return. Through the heartfelt emotions of the prodigal's father, we are provided a wide-open window on why Jesus was celebrating and graciously receiving sinners—and in turn the reason why we ourselves should be doing the same. *Read Luke 15:1–32.*

1. From v. 1, state the circumstances of the telling of these parables. (cf. Luke 7:34)

2. What problem(s) do the *"Pharisees and scribes"* (v. 2) have with what Jesus is doing? (cf. Luke 18:9–14)

3. According to the parables of the *Lost Sheep* and *Lost Coin* (vv. 3–10), how does God respond when one of His valued ones is lost?

   How does He react when He finds His lost one?

4. The third, and climatic parable, tells the story of a father and his two sons. Describe all the ways in which the younger son brings shame to his family. (vv. 11–13, 30)

5. How is every person's choice to sin like the younger son's choices? (cf. James 1:14–15)

Similarly, how is vv. 14–20a a picture of any person's repentance? (cf. Psalm 51:16–17)

6. Visualize the father's reaction upon seeing his younger son returning home (vv. 20b–24). How does he treat the son who insulted him and squandered his hard-earned wealth?

7. Using the father's welcome of his prodigal son as your model, how would you describe to a friend our Heavenly Father's forgiveness of the sinner who returns to Him?

8. Unwilling to join the celebration, the older son fumes outside the house (vv. 25–30). What do you notice in his language about his perspectives and attitude?

   How does the father respond to his older son's objections? (vv. 31–32)

9. For reasons that might be similar to the older son's, in what way(s) might the Heavenly Father's lavish forgiveness challenge our notions of fairness?

10. Ultimately, what kind of response is God seeking from us (and the Pharisees from vv. 2–3) when a sinner comes home?

11. What person can you demonstrate God's love and grace to this week? How will you do it?

Last Word: In our lesson we've stressed the point that we serve a Father in Heaven who joyfully showers His gracious forgiveness upon His repentant children. *"Let us celebrate,"* He shouts to the heavenly host, *"for this my son was dead, and is alive again; he was lost, and is found."*

Additionally, we've noted that we are called to emulate our Father's forgiveness. No doubt this can be hard, especially when we've been deeply hurt by another. But no matter how challenging it may be for us to forgive another person, that is no excuse for withholding mercy to the repentant. Rather, we should fearfully seek to *"Grow in the grace and knowledge of our Lord and Savior Jesus"* (2 Peter 3:18a). By pursuing spiritual maturity through a deeper knowledge of Christ and His grace we can continually move ever closer to forgiving as freely and graciously as our Heavenly Father has forgiven us.

Prayer: Ask God to help you take His words of instruction and example to heart so that you too will graciously forgive as freely as He does and celebrate the return of His lost children.

Lesson 2
Our Need for Forgiveness

Ephesians 2:1–10

There is a hymn we occasionally sing entitled, "I'm the One" (Roy Overholt). In this song we acknowledge that we were not present during Jesus' arrest and crucifixion. "But every time I sin on earth, I feel that I'm the one." Lyrically, this song challenges us to see the degree to which we could sin. "I'm the one who shouted 'crucify,' I'm the one who made that cross so high, I'm the one who stood and watched him die, What have I done I'm the one."

Think of the most evil person you have ever encountered. Do you think you would be capable of committing the same sinful crimes? Probably not because typically when we compare our sins to the offenses of others, our transgressions, at least to us, seem quite negligible. Nevertheless, God sees our sins in terms of an enormous debt we can never repay even if we live a thousand lives over. But, from the depths of His mercy, love, and grace He saves us; freely forgiving us of all our sins.

In our text, the apostle Paul gives us a focused picture of how far from God we once were and how powerfully He worked to restore us. Consequently, our own need for forgiveness becomes the most compelling source of strength for us to forgive others. *Read Ephesians 2:1–10.*

1. From vv. 1–3, how would you describe the spiritual nature of a person overpowered by sin?

2. Is there any way that you fall, or have fallen in the past, into the description of the person described in vv. 1–3? Explain.

3. Forgiveness of our *"trespasses and sins"* emerges from three aspects of God's nature: His mercy, love and grace (vv. 4–5). In your own words, briefly explain each quality.

4. Several passages vividly paint a picture of what God does with our forgiven sins: i.e. Psalm 103:12; Isaiah 43:25; and Micah 7:19. What do these images say to you about the extent of your forgiveness?

5. Furthermore, Paul describes forgiven people as being *"made alive," "raised," "seated"* with Christ and recipients of *"the immeasurable riches of His grace"* (vv. 5–7). What difference does the reality of your union with Christ make in your everyday life?

6. According to vv. 8–9, how does Paul confront the person who thinks they have earned God's forgiveness?

7. In what way(s) does a self-righteous spirit keep us from forgiving others? (cf. Luke 18:9–14)

8. Verse 10 is one of the central statements of Paul's teaching of the gospel of grace. Paraphrase what he is saying here?

9. How does knowing that you are God's *"handiwork"* or *"workmanship"* affect the way you think about:

    God—

    Yourself—

    Others –

10. Throughout this passage, Paul assures us of God's willingness to graciously forgive those who believe in Him. With that in mind, what can we do to assure other people of our willingness to forgive? (cf. Matthew 7:1–5)

What good work of forgiveness will you do this week? Tell a friend and ask them to hold you accountable.

Last Word: I firmly believe that there is a direct correlation between how we view our own need for forgiveness and our willingness to forgive others. Simply stated, the more we see our need for God's forgiveness, the more we'll forgive others. God has freely released each of us from a sin debt we could never repay. How much more should we do the same for others? Paul ends this passage with a call for the forgiven to remember we are pardoned people *"in Christ Jesus for good works which God prepared beforehand, that we should walk in them."* We don't do good works to earn God's mercy; we do good works because we have been changed by His grace. Godly behavior flows from a grace-centered heart. I can think of no better good work than sharing the love, mercy and grace of God with someone who has wronged you.

Prayer: Ask God to help you remember that you were once lost and separated from Him but through mercy, love and grace He forgave your sins. Pray for the power to forgive others.

Lesson 3

Confessing Our Sins

1 John 1:5—2:2

Have you ever kept a secret that was simply killing you to hold it inside? Maybe it was one of those good secrets such as an unannounced pregnancy or a surprise engagement. With your heart overflowing with joy you wanted to tell someone but couldn't. On the other hand, perhaps you harbored a bad secret —something that you hoped no one ever discovered, but deep down you wanted to confess to someone, anyone so you could unload the burden you carried. Thus, caught up in the vicious cycle of shame you remain silent and needlessly suffer. But there is a way to break free of the guilt you carry.

As I grow in the faith, I am more and more convinced that the basics of what God expects of us can be laid out rather simply. In triadic form, we are called to constantly walk in God's light, contritely confessing our sins, and thankfully accepting His gracious cleansing. Of these three, the humiliating task of contritely confessing our sins demands our focus because, to our spiritual hurt, we so often neglect this most humbling act. Its basic doctrine to affirm the Christian life cannot be lived without faith; but nor can it be lived without the acknowledgment our own sinfulness. *Read 1 John 1:5—2:2.*

1. What do you envision about God when you read: *"God is light, and in Him is no darkness at all"* (1:5)?

2. What mistaken view about one's lifestyle and relationship with God does John expose in 1:6, 8, 10?

   In your own words, explain how this can be done explicitly and / or passively.

3. What does John mean when he calls for believers to *"walk in the light"* (1:7) as opposed to *"walk[ing] in darkness"* (1:5, 6)?

4. If we *"walk in the light,"* doing what God commands, why do we need to continually rely on the blood of Jesus to purify us from all sin (1:7b)?

5. John states that he is writing these things to combat sin, but the reality is believers do sin, even grievously (2:1). In what way(s) does Matthew 26:41 and Romans 7:18–25 illustrate the tension between wanting to do right but failing to do so?

With v. 9, John turns to the issue of confessing our sins to God. Just as persistently *"walk[ing] in the light"* is an indication of belief in Christ, continual confession of our sins and ungodliness is an indication of salvation. The term *"confess"* means to say the same thing about sin as God does; that is to acknowledge His perspective about sin.

6. Select a few Bible verses and write out a short description of what God thinks about our sin.

7. Typically our confessions fall woefully short of expressing what God thinks of our sins. Why do you think we are reluctant at times to really acknowledge our sins to God?

8. Thankfully, God's promise of forgiveness rests on His *"faithful and just"* character (1:9; 2:1b–2; cf. Psalm 103:8–13). How can this truth give us strength to overcome our fears and confess our sin to Him?

9. Genuinely confessing our sins to God has practical effects on how we view others. Using Titus 3:1–7 as your model,

how would you describe the relational change that comes from God's forgiveness?

Additionally, James encourages us to *"confess [our] sins to one another"* (James 5:16). How might confession to another person help us and them?

Last Word: Silence brings enslavement, confession brings freedom. Freedom from the soul-enslaving effects of sin and its eternal consequences. Admitting our sin is the first step in repentance. It involves waking up to the fact that we have been deceiving ourselves and that our thoughts, words and deeds have been wrong. This process is described in Isaiah 55:6–7, *"Seek the Lord while He may be found; call upon Him while He is near; let the wicked forsake his way, and the unrighteous man his thoughts; let him return to the Lord, that He may have compassion on him, and to our God, for He will abundantly pardon."*

There is no doubt, confession is hard but the reward of spiritual freedom far outweighs the humility of saying we've done wrong. So, if you desire to "walk in the light" with God our Father, you'll have to humbly and continually confess your sins to Him.

Prayer: Ask God for help confessing your sins to Him. Then pour out your heart to your Father acknowledging your sins, transgressions and iniquities. Say the same thing about your sins as He has said. Then, with a clean heart accept His forgiveness.

Lesson 4

Accepting God's Forgiveness

Psalms 32, 51

With a trembling voice a friend confided, "When I think about all that I've done, the people I've hurt, and the terrible consequences I've caused, I become paralyzed by regret, shame, and guilt. I just don't think I can ever forgive myself for what I've done." Can you identify with this person's sentiment? I'm sure that on one level or another, we can understand such emotions.

Perhaps a well-meaning friend may have told you that forgiving yourself is the first step toward healing and recovery. The problem is, nowhere in the Scriptures do we find God instructing us to deal with our heartaches by forgiving ourselves. Rather, He urges us to humbly accept the gracious forgiveness He provides.

Like us, Israel's King David experienced the highs and lows of spiritual living. Psalms 32 and 51 both emerge from a spiritual low–point in his life. Psalm 51 was written shortly after God's prophet confronted the King over his sins of adultery and murder. Within its stanzas David acknowledges the horrendous nature of his sins and pleads for God's forgiveness. While on the other hand, the tone of Psalm 32 suggests a later more contemplative work of praise. Through these two Psalms we're challenged to accept the joy and freedom of the Lord's pardon. The question for us is will we humbly accept God's forgiveness? *Read Psalm 51 then 32.*

1. Looking back to 2 Samuel 11:1–27, briefly summarize the story of David's sin with Bathsheba and against Uriah.

2. In Psalm 51, David refers to his spiritual failures as *"transgression"* (v. 1), as *"sin"* (v. 2), *"evil"* (v. 4), and as *"iniquity"* (v. 9). How do each of these words describe different aspects of what David did?

3. As David refuses to confess his sin, God seeks to draw him back. What happens inwardly when one refuses to come clean with God and confess sin? (see 32:3–4; 51:8b)

4. Finally, God sends His prophet Nathan to confront David (2 Samuel 12:1–15). How does David respond to God?

   Let's explore three reasons why we might struggle to accept God's forgiveness, noting David's response as a model for us to follow.

First, sometimes we might struggle to accept God's free forgiveness because we try to earn His mercy. How does David demonstrate that one must rely wholly on God's grace for forgiveness? (51:1, 7–12, 14–15; cf. 32:5 with 51:16–17)

Second, at other times, we could simply refuse God's forgiveness because we can't understand why He would possibly pardon us. In your own words, briefly explain the nature of God's forgiving spirit as described in Isaiah 55:6–9.

Read Psalm 32:1–2, 10–11. How does David model a faithful reaction to God's incomprehensible forgiveness?

Third, we may struggle to accept God's forgiveness because we don't feel forgiven when we suffer the painful consequences of our sins. What ramifications does David suffer for his iniquities? (2 Samuel 12:10–11, 14)

5. Put yourself in David's sandals, what emotions do you think you would have wrestled with in the same situation?

6. Using Proverbs 3:11–12 and 2 Corinthians 12:7–10 as

your source, how would you help a friend cope with the negative consequences of sin that God allows into their lives?

7. Lastly, David vows to, *"teach transgressors [God's] ways"* (51:13; cf. 32:8–9). From your perspective, how would all that he endured enable him to better instruct others?

After this study, what will you be able to teach others from your own experience of forgiveness?

Last Word: David's story challenges us to accept God's forgiveness despite our own feelings. There's an old hymn we sing entitled, "Bring Christ Your Broken Life" (Thomas Chisholm). The song speaks to the struggling heart wrestling to accept God's forgiveness. The second verse is especially poignant:

> Bring [Christ] your every care if great or small–
> Whatever troubles you—O bring it all!
> Bring Him the haunting fears, the nameless dread
> Thy heart He will relive, and lift up they head.

Forgiveness isn't something you can give yourself; it is something Jesus has purchased for you. Let Him take away the regret, shame and guilt and *"Be glad in the Lord, and rejoice, O righteous, and shout for joy, all you upright in heart!"* (32:11).

The Father's grace and blessing are yours to enjoy. I urge you, accept God's forgiveness today and begin to live your life with a new found hope and joy.

Prayer: Ask God to create in you a heart that joyfully accepts His forgiveness, overcoming any and all doubts that might arise in our hearts.

Lesson 5

Saying I'm Sorry

Matthew 5:21–26

Whenever Micah has some playtime with his friends or cousins he will undoubtedly bonk one of them on the head, or take their toy away. On such occasions I will get to exercise my stern parent voice saying, "Micah, say you're sorry." As four-year-olds go, Micah can have a frustratingly stubborn will against apologizing. All of this makes me wonder how frustrating it must be to God when a grown adult, acting like a four-year-old, refuses to say, "I'm sorry."

Discord between people is inevitable. Therefore, nearly all of what the scriptures has to say about conflict is geared toward resolving issues to bring about peace and unity through forgiveness and reconciliation.

The apostle Paul instructs us, *"If possible, so far as it depends on you, live peaceably with all"* (Romans 12:18). In order to live out this directive, we'll have to honestly humble ourselves and say, "I'm sorry" to those we've hurt. In return, we'll also have to graciously say, "I forgive you" to those who've pained us. The question that all of us must answer is this, will we live out the high calling of our faith by humbly seeking peace or will we pridefully perpetuate discord? *Read Matthew 5:21–26.*

1. Look closely at Matthew 5:17–48 noting the repeated phrase, *"You have heard that it was said ... but I say ..."* What do you think Jesus means by these words?

2. In your own words, restate the Lord's teaching on murder and anger from vv. 21–22.

3. After establishing our culpability to angry thoughts and actions, why do you think Jesus would want us to seek reconciliation with someone we've offended before we offer our worship to God? (vv. 23–24; cf. 1 John 4:20–21)

4. Despite our Lord's teaching, we're often reluctant to seek to make amends with people we've wronged. From your perspective, list a couple of reasons why we act like this, along with how we can overcome these obstacles.

5. Jesus ends His teaching on reconciliation with a short parable illustrating the need for reconciliation (vv. 25–26). Elaborate on what might all be involved in *"Come[ing] to terms quickly"* (ESV) with someone you've wronged.

Now let's turn our attention to the other person in this equation … the one who has been hurt.

6. The apostle Paul exhorts us to, *"Be kind to one another, tenderhearted, forgiving one another, as God in Christ forgave you"* (Ephesians 4:32). In your own words, what does it mean to forgive those who have sinned against you?

7. What reasons have you used (or could you use) to resist forgiving another person?

   How would you counsel another Christian who came to you with these same reasons for not forgiving someone else?

8. Why is overcoming our excuses for not forgiving such a critical aspect of our walk of faith? (see Matthew 6:14–15; John 13:35; 17:20–23)

9. Considering what Jesus says in Matthew 6:14–15, what would happen if God forgave you in the exact the same manner you forgive others?

   Conversely, what would happen if you forgive others in the same graceful way God forgives you?

Last Word: Let's go back to the Sermon on the Mount and this time to the seventh beatitude, *"Blessed are the peacemakers"* Jesus says, *"for they will be called sons of God"* (Matthew 5:9). As we've seen demonstrated in our lesson, the Lord's teaching goes far beyond a merely peaceful disposition to an active attempt to *"make"* peace. It is a characteristic of God's true people to *"seek peace and pursue it"* (Psalm 34:14). All those who endeavor to promote peace are like the Father and are worthy to be called His children.

Do you want to be a child of God, reflecting the holy qualities of our Father? Then seek peace and unity. Make peace with those whom you have wronged. Forgive those who have wronged you. When we commit ourselves to this goal, we'll demonstrate to the world the love, grace, and mercy that is to be found in God our Father and Jesus Christ our Lord. And doesn't world need more love, grace, mercy?

Prayer: Ask God to give you a spirit that seeks peace and unity by being humble enough to say, "I'm sorry" and "I forgive."

Lesson 6

Saying You Hurt Me

Matthew 18:15–20

How do you typically handle disagreements or conflicts with another person? Are you the type who avoids conflict at all costs, unhealthily burying your emotions, while others go about their sinful ways? Or to the other extreme, are you the type of person who leaps at every opportunity to lash out at any and all offenders who dare cross your path. While these extreme approaches may be the norm with some, they resolve nothing and only make conflicts worse.

The Lord Jesus clearly calls for something much more loving and redemptive than timidly avoiding all confrontation or antagonizing others with a list of their wrongs. The main text for our study is Matthew 18:15–20. Unfortunately this passage is often associated only with the topic of church discipline. However, our passage is introduced with a theme of restoration, not condemnation. In the preceding five verses (vv. 10–14), we find Jesus' wonderful metaphor of a loving shepherd who goes to look for a wandering sheep and then rejoices when it is found.

So great is our Savior's concern for the matters of forgiveness and reconciliation, He has given us specific instructions about how to confront people who wound us—and what to do if they refuse to admit they're wrong. The challenge for us is to love people enough to confront them over their sins. *Read Matthew 18:15–20.*

1. First, let's note the wisdom statement of Proverbs 19:11. From your point-of-view, what is this maxim saying?

2. What guidelines would you use to counsel a friend on when it is wholly appropriate to *"overlook an offense"* committed against them?

3. When an offense can't or shouldn't be overlooked, what does Jesus first advise the offended to do? (v. 15)

4. The restoration of our sinning brother or sister is the goal of our one-on-one discussion. What insights do the following verses provide to help us achieve our aim? Matthew 7:1–5—Colossians 3:12–14—James 5:19–20 –

5. When our first attempts at reconciliation are unsuccessful, Jesus says to *"take one or two others along with you."* What

do you perceive to be the benefit(s) of involving others? (v. 16)

6. If all other efforts fail, what will hopefully be accomplished by taking the extreme measures of v. 17?

7. Jesus' words, *"If your brother sins against you"* (v. 15) directs His teaching to issues between Christians. Which of these principles might help us resolve issues with non–Christians?

8. According to vv. 18–20, what promises does Jesus make to those who are faithful in areas of pursuing reconciliation and resolving conflicts?

Now let's turn our attention to the other person in this equation … the one who has done wrong.

9. What is your typical response when someone confronts you over your faults?

10. How do passages such as Psalm 141:5, and Proverbs 27:6 challenge us to see reproof from others in a positive light?

11. Let's say that efforts to bring about restoration were successful. Scripture then says, *"bear fruit in keeping with repentance"* (Matthew 3:8). How will continuing to do this aid in reconciling ourselves to the one(s) we've wounded?

Last Word: By God's grace, many conflicts between Christians (and non-believers as well) can be resolved by simply talking personally and privately with someone who has wounded us. However, when personal efforts do not succeed, Jesus has given us a simple yet effective process for involving others who can promote understanding and agreement.

Remember, when our endeavors are carried out with prayer, wisdom, and reliance on the power of God's grace, the Father is pleased to use our efforts to promote peace. Do you have unresolved conflict from your past or present? Seek to honor God today by going to your brother or sister and by God's grace gain back your friend.

Prayer: Ask God to give you the courage to go to those who sin against you—and the humility to go with grace. Also, for the courage to admit our wrongs—and the humility to seek restoration.

Lesson 7

The Power of a Forgiving Spirit

Romans 12:14, 17–21

Peacemaking does not always go as smoothly as we would like. While some people, with honest hearts, readily make peace, others stubbornly and defensively resist our efforts to be reconciled. Sometimes they will become even more antagonistic, seeking new ways to mistreat us. Our human nature says to strike back at such people, or at the least to stop doing anything good for them. But what does God say?

At times, well-meaning Christians ask, "Do I have to forgive someone if they don't repent?" It's only natural to feel this way. However, this is the wrong question to ask because the negative nature of the query reflects a heart that's not inclined to want to forgive. Rather, a better question is, "What can I do to show my forgiving spirit to the one who won't repent?"

Scripture doesn't encourage a passive response to sin. Instead, we are taught that we should go on the offense—not to beat down or destroy our opponents, but to win them over to God and us through a loving, merciful, and forgiving spirit. This is the kind of heart and spirit our Lord seeks of us. Will we obey? *Read Romans 12:14, 17–21.*

1. In what way(s) are you tempted to respond to someone who hurts you and resist your pleas to repent?

2. What can we learn from 2 Corinthians 10:3–6 about the nature of the *unnatural* forgiving spirit Paul calls for in Romans 12:14, 17–21?

In our text, Paul outlines 5 principles to help us maintain a forgiving spirit with those who persistently resist our efforts to make peace.

I. Paul instructs us on the proper use of the tongue, *"bless those who persecute you"* (v. 14). What impact do you think doing this would have on our hearts?

II. Next, the apostle says to, *"give thought to do what is honorable in the sight of all"* (v. 17). In your own words, what does Paul mean by this? (cf. 1 Peter 2:12, 15; 3:14–16)

III. Paul writes, *"If possible, as far as it depends on you, live peaceable with all"* (v. 18). From your perspective, what does this look like or include as a display of a forgiving spirit?

Building on the previous question, do you think it's ever okay to pull back from actively making every effort possible to be reconciled to someone? Explain.

IV. We're called to *"never avenge [ourselves], but leave it to the wrath of God"* (v. 19). This can be difficult, why do you think believers struggle with this command?

V. Finally, instead of acting vengefully, we are called to care for our enemy's needs (v. 20a). Think of a time when someone treated you (or another person) like this. What was it like for everyone involved?

3. Paul promises that by doing good to our enemy we *"will heap burning coals on his head"* (v. 20b). Using reliable resources, briefly explain this peculiar phrase and the promise it holds.

4. The final words of our passage states, *"Do not be overcome by evil, but overcome evil with good"* (v. 21). What difference would it make in our responses to painful circumstances if we really believed evil could be overcome with good?

Last Word: The Lord's high standards for His followers grate against our me–first human nature. From a worldly perspective, the approach we've outlined seems naïve and appears to concede defeat, but God's ways are not the world's ways. There's no doubt about it, there is profound power in a forgiving spirit.

Applying these principles can be difficult, but God hasn't asked us to do something hard that He Himself hasn't already done. His life serves as an example that we are to follow, *"When He was reviled, He did not revile in return; when He suffered, He did not threaten, but continued entrusting himself to Him who judges justly"* (1 Peter 2:23). Since Jesus chose to display a forgiving spirit when dealing with His enemies, even crying from the cross *"Father forgive them"* (Luke 23:34), we should do the same.

Offering our enemies a forgiving spirit is always worth the effort, because God delights to work in and through us as we serve Him, seeking to make peace with those around us.

Prayer: Think of someone who has recently mistreated you. Pray for that person by name seeking God's blessing for them and asking Him for the strength you need to serve that person with acts of mercy.

Lesson 8

The Danger of an Unforgiving Spirit

Matthew 18:21–35

Our society is riddled with rancor and bitterness. We almost consider it a normal response to life. Unfortunately, this has bled into the life of believers to the point that an unforgiving spirit is an all too common attitude among Christians.

The Hebrew writer warns us to, *"See to it … that 'no root of bitterness' springs up and causes trouble, and by it many become defiled"* (12:15). The author is alluding to Deuteronomy 29:18, which describes one who defiles themselves by turning away from the one true God to pursue false gods. From our point of view, the one who allows bitterness and an unforgiving spirit to take root in their hearts has turned from God to worship at the altars of the false gods of hurt feelings, resentment, and anger. The longer we serve these self-made idols, the more difficult it becomes for us to break free. We must recognize, that in this state we stand under God's judgment. His curses will be upon us and *"the Lord will blot our [our] name from under heaven"* (Deuteronomy 29:20).

But you can be free, let's learn how together. *Read Matthew 18:21–35.*

1. What is your typical response when you are asked to forgive someone for the same offense several times over? Explain why you have this attitude

2. Looking at v. 21, do you think Peter had a special reason for asking Jesus how often he was required to forgive the person who sins against him? Explain your answer.

3. What does Jesus' answer tell you about how forgiveness operates in His kingdom? (v. 22)

4. To further illustrate His teaching, Jesus tells the *Parable of the Unforgiving Servant*. The parable opens with a *king "who wished to settle accounts with his servants"* (v. 23). Describe the predicament one servant found himself in. (vv. 24–26)

5. Out of pity, the king graciously forgives his servant's enormous debt. Then what unconscionable act does the servant commit upon leaving the kings presence? (vv. 28–30)

For easy comparison, let's put the two debts in the simple terms of dollars. In that case, the first servant owed his master something on the lines of $62.6 Million while he was owed a mere $100. Boiled down, the first servant was forgiven $626,000 and then choked his fellow slave for one measly dollar

6. The king, upon hearing a report about the first servant's actions (v. 31) promptly summons him. What is the point of his indictment in vv. 32–33?

7. This parable is obviously not about how to treat people who owe you money. What do the two debts represent in our lives?

   What contrast does Jesus want us to draw?

8. It can be difficult to detect bitterness in our hearts. From your experience, what are some of the telltale evidences that hurt has morphed into an unforgiving spirit?

9. Because the servant failed to reciprocate his master's mercy, he was handed over to the *"torturers"* (v. 34). What could some of those tormentors be in our lives if we have an unforgiving spirit?

10. How does a failure to forgive affect our capacity to experience God's love and grace? (v. 35; Ephesians 4:29–32)

Last Word: My intention is not to load you down with guilt or insert additional blame into a situation that's already charged with hurt and emotion. But if we want to be free—free from our tormentors, free to enjoy God's forgiveness—then we first have to acknowledge the depths that unforgiveness has reached in our lives. We have to recognize the damage it's caused and can cause. And we have to deal with the fact that our unforgiveness is a sin, just as the original offense committed against us was. No worse of a sin, but certainly no less of one.

As I've tried to bring God's word to bear on the subject of forgiveness, my desire was not to add to your burden but to spare you more pain. I long for you to enjoy the blessing, the freedom, and the transformational power of walking in the light of God's gracious forgiveness. I pray the Lord's blessings be upon you as you forgive one another as God in Christ forgave you.

Prayer*: Thank God for forgiving your enormous debt of sin. Ask Him to root out any bitter unforgiving spirit in your heart.*

Clay's Bio

Clay Gentry is the preacher at the Jackson Heights Church of Christ in Columbia, Tennessee. He shares his life with his wife of 25 years, Shelly, a reading specialist at Columbia Academy, and their four children: Isaac, Lillie, Micah, and Anna. When he's not in the pulpit, you might find him exploring an old cemetery, hiking scenic trails, repairing a car or two, or simply relaxing with a good book and a cup of coffee. *(He's also a huge Elvis fan, and secretly believes he can channel The King while singing karaoke. But that's a story for another time.)*

www.ingramcontent.com/pod-product-compliance
Lightning Source LLC
Chambersburg PA
CBHW040323050426
42453CB00017B/2441